Reflections from the Heart

A collection of Poems & Songs

Sandy King

WestBow Press books may be ordered through booksellers or by contacting:

WestBow Press
A Division of Thomas Nelson & Zondervan
1663 Liberty Drive
Bloomington, IN 47403
www.westbowpress.com
844-714-3454

ISBN: 978-1-6642-6751-0 (sc)
ISBN: 978-1-6642-6753-4 (hc)
ISBN: 978-1-6642-6752-7 (e)

Library of Congress Control Number: 2022909576

Print information available on the last page.

WestBow Press rev. date: 7/27/2022

WESTBOW
PRESS®
A DIVISION OF THOMAS NELSON
& ZONDERVAN

Foreword

"*To be a poet is a condition, not a profession.*" by Robert Graves
I have always loved poetry. I still remember a poem I made up when I was 8.

> "*I'm a little sailor always to be
> kind and true, just for you.
> I'm a little sailor always to be
> glad to work for my country.*"

This passion was encouraged by my sixth-grade teacher, Mrs. Burns. I wrote many poems that year but, alas, they did not survive adulthood. She told my mother at a parent-teacher conference that I had a gift for writing poems. I have always kept the compliment close to my heart.

I guess the ability came naturally since we have copies of poems written by both of my paternal grandparents. Over the years of a very busy life, I have written some rhymes, but they were few and far between.

When my husband, Ron, and I retired from our jobs in Juneau, Alaska, we moved to the Kenai Peninsula where our daughter and family live. Their house is 16 miles from the nearest town. In Juneau, I was the director of a preschool, gave piano lessons, and played for many community events. I enjoyed hiking, our Church and friends. Here, I was in the middle of the Alaskan wilderness.

God used this quiet time of my life to draw me closer to him. He taught me how to be Christ's follower, not just do Christianity. I fell in love with Him all over again. Then, God reignited the passion from my childhood of writing poetry.

My prayer is that God will use these poems to bless you, and to speak truth into your life.

Sandy's Song

I used to play a tune filled with discord.
I wondered why I was born on this earth.
Then I met Jesus; I gave Him my life;
And He gave me a song of new birth.

It's a song that has the sweetest melody,
For it tells of Christ coming from above,
Of His death on Calvary's cruel tree,
Of His care, grace, and wondrous love.

There may come situations I don't understand,
But the melody is there, just the same.
When I look up into my Savior's face;
I can't help singing praises to His name.

He writes a song of love upon my heart.
He writes a song that never shall depart.
He writes a song that makes my whole world bright,
And keeps me singing in the night.

Table of Contents

Relational

Love is caring.
Love is sharing.
Love is bearing one another's burdens.
Love is giving.
Love is living
To please the Lord.

Our Song

Our life is like a song to sing
in our own tone and key.
Each life we touch inscribes a note
that forms the melody.
God decides the chording for the song
to bear our name.
Each will have a special sound;
no two can be the same.
So when someone we love departs,
in memory we find,
Their song plays on within the hearts
of those they leave behind.

Who

Gave thanks to God when I was born;
Continued to pray for me each morn;
Walked the floor when I was sick;
Gave castor oil to fix me quick;
Dried my tears when I was sad;
Gave a scold when I was bad;
Cleaned, washed and ironed, too;
A hundred chores would gladly do;
Cooked healthy meals to keep me fit;
Crocheted afghans, and also knit;
Caring for others was how she lived;
Following a creed to give and give.
When Jesus calls and her life is done;
A crown in heaven she will have won.

    Who is this Saint?
    It is no other
    Than the Godly woman
    I call MOTHER.

I wrote this poem in October 2003, on an
airplane traveling from Alaska to Washington
to see my folks. I had no idea mom would be
with Jesus five days later. I was able to share
it with her the next day, and she was blessed.

I'm Committed

There are stars in my eyes,
Tuxedos and lace.
My head's in the clouds;
We've a honeymoon place.
I'M COMMITTED

A baby already,
Back to school we go.
How can we do this?
God will help us we know.
I'M COMMITTED

Graduation at last,
Another baby here.
We are going to move
To Alaska, oh dear!
I'M COMMITTED

A strange place to live,
And I miss my mother.
But we will survive
With God and each other.
I'M COMMITTED

There're babies and bottles
And staying up nights.
We don't think the same;
Sometimes we have fights.
I'M COMMITTED

We've seen joy and sorrow
Down through the years.
The laughter is mixed with
Frustration and tears.
I'M COMMITTED

Our love has grown strong;
It's noble and fine.
Since I am all yours,
And you are all mine.
WE'RE COMMITTED

This poem was written after our 15th anniversary. I firmly believe its theme is the key to a long lasting marriage.

4

Let the Children Come

As I reflect on the different children's ministries that I have enjoyed, this poem comes to mind. It was written as a song for the preschool I directed.

Verse 1

See the little children,
They're curious and smart,
Playful, mischievous,
But with such tender hearts.
See the little children,
Souls for whom Christ died.
He dearly loves the children
And calls them to His side.

Verse 2

See the little children,
Their laughter and their tears,
Shining eyes, button noses,
Precious through the years.
See the little children,
Their hugs, their hurts and sighs.
They grow up so quickly,
The time is passing by.

Chorus

"Let the children come to Me",
Are Jesus' words today.
Let them see the love of Christ
In all we do and say.
"Let the children come",
Is a command we must obey.
Let's reach out to the children
So they will know the way.

Ending

Let us tell the children
That Jesus is the way.

Children

Tomorrow there'll be no:

Toothpaste in the sink,
Socks on the floor,
Sand in the shoebox,
Legos by the door.

Spills on the table,
Music on the bench,
Videos on the cabinet,
Hampers with a stench.

Skates on the rug,
Shoes on the stairs,
Tubs filled with toys,
Baby dolls and bears.

Clothes will be ironed,
No rips or stains,
Shoes will be shined,
Life will be sane.

But I will miss:

The twinkling eye,
The dimpled smile,
The sitting down
To read awhile.

The trusting hand,
The button nose,
The listening ear,
The restless toes.

The time to talk,
The time to see,
The time to walk,
The time to be.

The lessons taught,
The family game,
Without these things
Life's not the same.

They will all be gone tomorrow,
So, I will enjoy today.

Grandkids

Grandkids are the best!
Though with them I never rest:
Eating, playing,
Singing, praying.
I just love the stress!

Their antics I don't mind.
With them I always find
Laughter and hugs,
Stories on rugs,
They help me unwind.

I want to let them know:
Grandpa and I love them so.
Our lives we would give,
If it would help them live.
May we always God's love show.

To My Child Far Away

There are times when I really wish we were closer.
We can't chat over a hot drink.
I can't make your favorite meal.
I can't share your daily joys and sorrows.
I can't lend my shoulder to cry on or lean on.
I can't reach out and feel your embrace.
BUT I CAN PRAY FOR YOU!

Often during the day, I visit you with my prayers.
I think of you awakening, and ask for strength in a new day.
I picture you at your activities, and ask for safety and peace.
I see you at home and pray you will use time wisely.
I ask for rest and renewal as you settle in to bed.
But my constant prayer is that your eyes will look up;
That you will walk close to GOD,
WHO LOVES YOU SO MUCH.

I wrote this poem when our eldest child left the nest.
The title has changed over the years to children and grandchildren.

Friends

God has a wonderful plan,
A precious gift to send,
Someone to share the journey,
And so He gives a friend.

A friend is an encourager
Who will lend a helping hand.
She will laugh or cry with you,
And try to understand.

A friend takes time to listen
With a heart that really cares.
She also takes the time to talk,
And keeps you in her prayers.

A friend will love to celebrate
The joys that life will bring.
This multiplies the blessings,
And makes the soul take wing.

And friends are friends forever
If they follow God above;
For He will do the bonding
With true Agape love.

God's Dependables

God's dependables,
you see them everywhere.
They show up when needed,
always without fanfare.

They are the body of Christ;
His eyes, hands, and feet.
They share the love of Jesus
with everyone they meet.

They might give a hug,
a wise word or smile.
They may sit beside you
and listen for a while.

Their house is always open
if someone needs a bed.
Food, clothes, or money,
they give as Jesus said.

They try to be available
to walk, talk or pray,
read, teach, sing,
or help in anyway.

They are living sermons,
true in words and deeds.
God can depend on them
to follow where He leads.

I Don't Need to Know

My nephew and niece, Nick and Audreyanna went home to be with the Lord. This poem was written because it is hard to understand, this side of eternity, God's plans for our lives.

I don't need to know the reason
For sorrows that come my way,
For Christ is close beside me,
    and in His arms, I stay.

I don't need to know the whys
For the trials that life will bring,
For God will always give me
Songs in the night to sing.

God uses His Living Word,
Family and friends so dear,
A meal, a hug, a helping hand,
To show that He is near.

He's the Father of all comfort
And every pain He shares.
He understands our heartaches
And every burden bears.

I trust in His sovereignty,
And rest in His boundless love.
All mysteries will be revealed
When we reach heaven above.

Companionship

Fifty years ago,
I made a vow to you,
That I would love and cherish,
And always to you be true.

You asked if I would be
Your wife, lover, and friend;
The mother of our children,
Together until life's end.

I was young and in love,
So I quickly answered yes.
I had no way of knowing
How much I would be blessed.

You have been my companion,
All these many years.
We walked life's road together
In spite of heartaches and fears.

I look across a room,
I see a smile just for me.
I'm warm inside just to know
I'm loved so constantly.

It's an irreplaceable gift,
All the time we share.
The walks, talks, and cuddles
That let me know you care.

You tell me you see beauty
Although I'm old and gray.
You help and protect me
And kiss me every day.

Now we have become
One body, mind and soul.
Christ holds us together
For He has made us whole.

Seasonal

Bloom where you are planted,
Don't wish you could stray.
New flowers can keep growing,
No matter where you stay.
Bloom where you're planted,
Hope you will be granted.
Bloom where you are planted today.

A New Year

What a precious gift, an entire year,
Filled with joy or pain, peace or fear.

52 weeks in which to grow,
Sometimes fast and sometimes slow.

365 days to use,
For good or bad, as I choose.

525,600 minutes to embrace,
With hectic steps or a steady pace.

31,536,000 seconds,
To look to God and follow as He beckons.

Thank you, Father, for an empty slate,
A brand new path, with a brand new gate.

May I listen to the Spirit and go where led,
Live in Your truth, from Your Word be fed.

Make me an example of mercy and grace,
To cherish each glimpse of a loved one's face.

Give me strength and courage to carry-on.
In my heart, may there always be a song.

I give you this year, minutes, seconds and days.
Help me to be faithful and walk in Your ways.

Upon arriving in Juneau in September of 2016, I was traversing East Glacier Trail within the hour. It is my favorite trail and inspired the following poem.

The Dappled Trail

I love the trail, the dappled trail,
When all the trees are green,
With verdant hues more brilliant
Than I have ever seen.
Ferns, moss, and flowers
Lift faces to the sun.
Leaves adorn the branches,
As over the path I run.

I love the trail, the dappled trail,
When all the trees are gold.
The filtered sun glitters,
And is marvelous to behold.
Down the gentle hillside,
Covered with leaf and rock,
I hear a crunchy cadence,
As over the path I walk.

I love the trail, the dappled trail,
When all the trees are white.
A glistening, silvery snowfall
Covers everything in sight.
Icicles sparkle; branches droop;
Bears have long gone to bed.
Cleats assure a safe journey,
As over the path I tread.

I love the trail, the dappled trail,
At every time of year.
For in the quiet of the woods,
I can always hear
The voice of God the Creator
Speak softly to my soul.
I join the trees in worship,
As over the path I stroll.

Contentment

Like a bee sipping on nectar;
Like a dog enjoying a treat;
Like a bear feasting on honey;
So I bow at my Savior's feet.

Like a swan swimming on a lake;
Like a robin sitting on its nest;
Like a baby in its mother's arms;
So I come to Jehovah for rest.

Like rainbows after the rain;
Like fields when flowers abound;
Like clouds high in the sky;
So contentment in Christ is found.

Content amidst the chaos;
Content in spite of strife;
Content through the suffering;
As I travel the path of life.

For Jesus walks beside me,
And lightens every load.
My hand is firmly clasped in His,
As we journey the rugged road.

Contentment has always been a struggle for me. Whether it was circumstances, looks, abilities, opportunities, etc, the grass often looked greener elsewhere. God continues to teach me to be content wherever I am planted.

Autumn Memories

Let's hear it for fall!
The best season of all!
The colors are grander,
Orange, red and amber,
On bushes and trees so tall.

The weather is such a delight;
Warm day and frosty night.
It's south the geese fly.
They honk their goodbye,
As they pass out of our sight.

See all the good things to eat!
Berries and fruits are so sweet.
Preserving the crops,
The job never stops.
But in winter, what a treat!

Activities fill up the days:
Lost in a muddy corn maze,
Cut the right places
To make pumpkin faces.
At the fireside, watch the blaze.

It's the season for the State Fair,
With booths and stalls everywhere.
The veggies are big,
And so is the pig.
Check out the rides if you dare.

By the light of the harvest moon,
And the call of the lonely loon.
We'll take a hayride
With friends by our side,
While singing a merry tune.

Thanksgiving to God we bring.
Praise to His Name we will sing.
For this bountiful land,
With vistas so grand,
Our prayers will ever take wing.

Household Blessings

Today, on Thanksgiving, I look around and see
Many things I take for granted. Lord, they are gifts from thee.

I thank you for our front room with piano, couches, chairs,
TV, tables, and recliner, to relax away our cares.

I thank you for a kitchen, with dishes, pots and pans,
Refrigerator, oven, and pantry filled with cans.

I thank you for our bedrooms: beds with pillows soft and wide,
For dressers and for closets, to keep our clothes inside.

I thank you for our bathrooms. What would we do without
Toilets, sinks and showers? We need them without a doubt.

These are a tiny picture of Your tender, loving care.
May I be ever thankful, and all Your blessings share.

Thanksgiving is a special day to think about God's goodness. I am very thankful for the big things in life - friends, family, creation, etc.; but am not as apt to acknowledge little, everyday blessings.

Deeper Meaning of Christmas

When children think of Christmas, it means Santa Claus and toys.
It's a time of giving gifts and singing carols of joy.
To some people Christmas means candlelight and trees,
And to others still it means food and festivities.

We all know that Christmas is the best time of the year.
It's a time of showing love to those whom we hold dear.
But on that day God's only Son was sent from heaven above.
He was born, and He died, that we might know His love.

Chorus
There's a deeper, deeper meaning to Christmas.
Do you know, do you care, that it's true?
There's a deeper, deeper meaning to Christmas.
Christ, the Savior, came to earth for you.

Bridge
Now He lives, victorious over death.
For His love is so very strong.
He offers the gift of salvation.
Why do you linger so long?

You'll know the deeper, deeper meaning of Christmas.
You'll have the Christ of Christmas in your heart.
You'll know the deeper, deeper meaning of Christmas.
And this joy will never from you depart.

Presents

All through my house, what do I see?
Presents, presents, presents, that loved ones gave to me.

Pictures of family, plaques with the Word,
Bells with the sweetest sounds you've ever heard.

Candles and doilies, a delicious hard cheese,
Mugs, quilts and candy as sweet as you please.

Presents for birthdays, and holidays, too.
Presents for thank you for all that you do.

Presents for get well, we do miss you so.
Presents for goodbye. Do you have to go?

But the greatest present there ever could be,
Was when Jesus was born for you and for me.

He came to this world and died in our place,
To give us the gift of salvation and grace.

We must but accept and walk in His way.
Love, joy and peace in our hearts then will stay.

Winter

Through my window shines
God's wonderful world of white.
Sparkling snowflakes
submerge the scenery in sight.

I softly sing a song
as I slip into my shoes.
With my canine companion,
I cavort as I choose.

We follow fleet footsteps
on the forest floor.
We spend magical moments
making memories to store.

Though it's brisk and bright,
the break time is laudatory,
For God's great grandeur,
I give Him all the glory.

Inspirational

HOPE

H – happily walking
O – onward
P – placing my trust in Jesus
E – every moment

Believe

When you look at creation,
The vast expanse of space,
Choreography for every star,
Each galaxy in its place;
Fish, fowl and flora,
Animals of every kind,
Tiny electrons in atoms
Orbit as God designed.
Does it not birth belief?

When you look at Mt. Calvary,
And view Jesus' love portrayed.
Legions of angels were ready,
But on the cross He stayed.
Enduring beatings and mocking,
Suffering untold agony;
He willingly gave up His life
So from sin we could be free.
Does it not birth belief?

When you look at the empty tomb,
No body where He had lain,
And angels proclaim, "He's alive!"
Three days after He was slain.
Peter and John and the women
Tell everyone that will hear.
Thomas touches Jesus' scars;
All doubts just disappear.
Does it not birth belief?

When you look at my life,
Touched by Jesus' love,
Given a hope and a future
That only comes from above.
God took my wounded soul,
With His Spirit did impart,
A new life of joy and peace
Into my repentant heart.
I pray that you can believe.

You Love Me

Verse 1
You know my days;
when I rise and when I sleep.
You know my heart;
when I laugh and when I weep.
You know my thoughts;
the shallow and the deep.
For You love me.

Verse 2
You know my fears,
and hear me when I call.
You know my strengths,
for You gave them all.
You know my sins,
and forgive me when I fall.
For You love me.

Chorus
Yes, You love me,
I can't begin to comprehend
how You love me,
In spite of all I've done and been.
Your love is wider, higher,
deeper than the sea.
I can only thank You
that it reaches even me.

Bridge
And though I don't know why,
I know that You love me.
For you took my place
when You died on Calvary.

Come and Dine

My Master gently calls me.
My child, you are mine.
My table is spread with plenty.
Come sit with Me and dine.

Don't settle for worldly food,
So bitter, tasteless, and dry.
You will find no nourishment
In scraps that won't satisfy.

My bread from heaven will satiate
The deep hunger of your soul.
My water of life will surely quench
Your thirst and make you whole.

My meat of the Word will strengthen
Your body and your mind.
My manifold fruit of the Spirit
Is of the sweetest kind.

Linger long at my buffet;
Partake of delectable fare.
We will talk, laugh, and feast
As companionship we share.

Walking in the Spirit

Love for God and fellow man,
Joy means trust in Jesus' plan,
Peace no problem can withstand,
If the Spirit's in charge of your soul.

Gentleness in work and play,
Goodness visible all the day,
Patience in all you do and say,
If the Spirit's in charge of your soul.

Meekness puts others before you,
Faith believes in what God will do.
Self-control shows excesses are few,
If the Spirit's in charge of your soul.

Chorus
Are you walking in the Spirit?
Is the fruit of your life love,
joy, peace and gentleness?
These only come from God above.
You'll have goodness, patience,
meekness, also faith and self-control.
These traits will be evidenced,
If the Spirit's in charge of your soul.

Trust

Trust is a child
who takes his father's hand,
and says I will follow,
though I don't understand.

Trust is moving forward
when all prospects seem dim.
It's clinging to God's promises
and holding fast to them.

Trust is knowing
God is in control,
even when circumstances
extract a dreadful toll.

Trust is believing,
through pain and loss,
remembering Jesus suffered
when dying on the cross.

Trust is laying on the altar
all that is so dear,
for the Lord will carry me,
and calm my every fear.

Trust is relinquishing
what seems to be my rights,
for I must keep heaven
and eternity in my sights.

Trust will keep me focused
until I see God's Son,
hear Him speak my name,
and say, "My child, well done."

Finding Joy

We all seek the answer,
where can joy be found?
Is it given by pleasure,
or treasure in the ground?

Do circumstances dictate
the emotions that we feel?
Must relationships be perfect
to know joy that is real?

Joy can come in trials,
through promises we share.
Joy comes from success,
when we choose to dare.

Joy comes from children
following a righteous path.
Joy comes from sharing
a kind word or a laugh.

Jesus, Others, then You,
spells joy all the day through.
When Jesus gets first place,
true joy will surely find you.

Forgiveness

How can I forgive
When I hurt so bad?
I feel like I have lost
Any joy I ever had.
How could it have happened?
I'm in such pain.
How can I go on,
And trust someone again?

While volunteering at Solid Rock Junior
Camp, the story of Corrie Ten Boom was
highlighted. I was privileged to read chapters
from Keeper of the Angel Den.

It was a reminder of her incredibly powerful
message of forgiveness. Here's my poem that
addresses this thorny topic.

Jesus knows your hurts;
He carried all your sins.
When dying on the cross,
He asked the Father to forgive.
Since He has forgiven you,
You must forgive others, too.
Then you will know His peace
And will be made anew.

Let it go --- Give it to God,
The bitterness, guilt and shame.
Let it go --- Give it to God,
The anger, vengeance and blame.
Let it go --- Give it to God,
Trust in His powerful name.
Surrender your hurts to Jesus.
You will never be the same.

Faith vs Fear

Faith is believing
that God remains in charge.
His providence controls
situations small and large.

Fear gives way to worry
about problems that abound.
They appear enormous;
no solution can be found.

Faith walks through the fire
without a burning smell.
Eyes fixed on Jesus
know all will turn out well.

Fear always trembles
behind doors locked up tight.
Shaken and shattered,
it shivers in the night.

Faith looks for promises
that are heaven sent.
It can find an answer
though resources are spent.

Fear scorns courage,
to opportunity is blind.
It lives with discouragement,
and strength will never find.

Put your faith in Jesus
for He knows what's best.
Put your fear behind you
to find peace and rest.

Motives

Why do you do the things you do?
Do you mostly do what amuses you?
Do you rely on feelings to direct your actions?
Do you lose focus when there are distractions?
Do you often try to manipulate?
Do you find it hard to activate?
Do you sometimes strive to draw a crowd?
Do you find by others you are cowed?

Why do you say the things you say?
Do you have to argue to get your own way?
Do you build others up or tear them down?
Do the words you say have a gentle sound?
Do you always think you must be right?
Do you set others straight by picking a fight?
Do you engage your mouth before your brain?
Do you have a tendency to complain?

We need to stop and evaluate,
Take some time to contemplate,
The motive behind our words and deeds,
And the destination to which it leads.
God says that whatever we do or say,
Should bring Him glory in every way.
We need to think before we act or speak.
Pleasing God is what we should seek.

Just Obey

When you hear a voice give a command to you;
You know that it is God. What do you do?

Do you refuse, whine, or pretend not to hear?
Or do you tune your ear to the Savior who's near?

Do you make excuses-too busy, tired or weak?
Or do you quickly stop and listen to Him speak?

Does your spirit bristle? Do you argue or rebel?
Or do you calmly submit and know life will be well?

Do you get distracted, fearful, or bored?
Or do you remember that He is your Lord?

Our heavenly Father knows what's good for us each day.
He will keep his promises. Why don't you just obey?

Be Quiet and Pray

It comes to your attention,
Many things need fixed.
You offer up solutions,
But often they are nixed.

You know that your advice
Would help the one in need.
You know it would be smart
For them to let you lead.

You feel that no one listens
To the things you have to say.
It is time to trust the Lord;
Just be quiet and pray.

There's a time to speak a word,
But it must be Spirit led.
For you may hurt feelings,
And regret the things you said.

God's the one who changes hearts,
And makes the blind to see.
He knows their inward motives,
And also their destiny.

Believe in His promises.
Know He will make a way.
Jesus has the answers.
Just be quiet and pray.

Backseat Driving

Lord, please do the driving.
I give you full control
Of my mind and body,
My heart and my soul.

You take the front seat;
I will sit behind.
You choose the way;
I will never mind.

But go by a straight road
With no dips or curves.
Not too fast or slow,
And never, ever swerve.

Be sure the sun is shining,
No rain clouds are in sight.
We will go by daylight,
So we can rest at night.

I'll be the one to tell you
When to stop and go,
When to make a turn,
Just so you will know.

I want to know how long
Before we will be there.
I would like refreshments,
And a more comfortable chair.

Onward we will journey
In our lovely automobile.
I'll sit in the backseat,
While You take the wheel.

A few years ago, I realized that I was spending too much time playing two games on my phone. I was robbing myself of valuable moments that could be used in more profitable enterprises physically, mentally or spiritually. So my New Year's resolution was to delete the apps and move on. This song reflects my true desire to use the God-given gift of time.

This Moment

Verse 1
This moment never comes again.
This moment will soon be past.
Life is just a vapor that appears and then is gone.
Only what is done for Christ will last.

Verse2
This moment, what will you do?
This moment, can Christ be seen in you?
We will be accountable for every word and deed.
Use them wisely for the moments are so few.

Chorus
I have this moment I hold in my hand.
God has given a choice to me.
I can waste it and lose it on things of this world,
Or I can give it to God, and I'll keep it for eternity.

When we retired and moved from Juneau in 2011, Ron looked at it as the beginning of a new life without the pressures of work; an opportunity to explore new horizons. My journey of acceptance is documented by this poem.

New Life

I'm at a new chapter.
My youth is behind.
My body grows weaker,
And so does my mind.
But the lessons I've learned
Through toil and tears,
Need to be shared
In the remaining years.

The Bible assures me
I can bloom in old age.
I have new life in Christ
Even in this stage.
I rest in God's presence.
Nothing can destroy
The peace that He gives;
Contentment and joy.

New life in Christ,
Each day is a chance,
To have a fresh start,
To take a bold stance.
No matter the years,
Be they many or few,
This is the question:
Is Christ shining through you?

Printed in the United States
by Baker & Taylor Publisher Services